EXCITED

Liverpool, t[...]
turns out a[...]
1914, to we[...]
acquisition – the [...]
flagship RMS Aquitania – 49,640 gross tons,
901 ft long, 97 ft wide, with a draft of 36 ft,
10 decks, 3,230 passengers and powered by
direct drive Parsons steam turbines driving
four propellers at a speed of 23 knots

Roll Call

Written by: Peter Elson

Design & Production: Vicky Andrews
Cover Design: Colin Harrison / Ben Renshaw

Pictures: Mirrorpix, Cunard

With special thanks to:
Lorna Gouldie, Special Collections and Archives,
University of Liverpool;
Peter Head; Paul Louden-Brown; Patricia Rainford

Trinity Mirror Media

Managing Director: Ken Rogers
Publishing Director: Steve Hanrahan
Senior Editor: Paul Dove
Executive Art Editor: Rick Cooke
Heritage Editor: Harri Aston
Senior Marketing Executive: Claire Brown
Sales and Marketing Manager: Elizabeth Morgan
Senior Sales Executive: Karen Cadman

Business Development Manager / Advertising
Will Beedles 0151 239 5949

Printed by Buxton Press

ISBN 9781908695864

Contents

AQUITANIA

CELEBRATING CUNARD'S 'SHIP BEAUTIFUL'

SHIP BEAUTIFUL

The visit of Queen Victoria to Merseyside in 2014 is a fitting celebration for the 100th anniversary of Aquitania's maiden voyage from Liverpool to New York. Her legacy remains a strong presence in the current Cunard fleet and she will always be remembered as the 'Ship Beautiful'

Was there ever a lovelier name for a ship than Aquitania?

A familiar sentiment as in so many minds her euphonious name, taken from the richest province of Roman Gaul and translating as 'Land of the Waters', epitomises this elegant ocean palace. In Aquitania's syllables you hear the paw of the Atlantic lapping against her high and handsome hull sides as her rapier bow cuts through the swell.

Conceived in Liverpool when the city was at its maritime and mercantile zenith a century ago, RMS Aquitania was the third and final, and ultimately most successful, vessel in Cunard Line's plan to create a trio of high-speed passenger and mail superliners - 'The Big Three' - linking the United Kingdom with the United States with a weekly service.

Not only did Aquitania outlive her half-sisters Lusitania and Mauretania by decades, she rode the oceans and the changing fortunes and fashions of the world's politics and trade in war and peace, like the great lady she was. Arguably, no ship other than Aquitania was so revered in the history of Cunard Line, apart from QE2, which pipped her longevity by just four years.

Dubbed 'the Ship Beautiful' in respect of her exquisite public interiors, she was also the 'Ship Lucky', the only great liner to serve in and survive both world wars.

Having always been mad about ships, my first experience of Aquitania was as an eight-inch long Tri-ang Minic die cast model, a holiday present bought by my parents at a Llandudno toy shop. These were the days when toy makers and youngsters thought it perfectly satisfying as a pastime to push inanimate miniature metal ships around on a jade-green coloured rippled polythene sea.

But even back then at the age of seven or eight years I could tell there was something

different about Aquitania. Almost all of Minic's accurately rendered fine little models were based on post-war ships and, even though scaled down to 1:1200, I realised Aquitania's design was clearly from an earlier age, with her long lean hull and counter stern. After all, what ship needed four tall funnels?

This was clearly a statelier, grander and more upright representative of a confident era that perfectly fitted Rudyard Kipling's refrain that the liner is a lady.

Affection can also be measured in the nicknames bestowed and Aquitania was no exception. In fact, these various names reflected her longevity, going from 'The World's Wonder Ship' and 'The Ship Beautiful' to 'Old Irrepressible', 'The Grand Old Lady' and 'Old Granny'. To her crews she was simply 'the Aqui', also an example of the Liverpudlian desire for diminutives.

In a career spanning 36 years, she steamed three million miles and carried 1,200,000 passengers, becoming one of the most exceptional ships of all time.

This is her story as told in the centenary year of her birth...

ELEVATED

Aquitania is high and dry and under repair in the Floating Dry Dock, Southampton

NEW START

Aquitania anchored in the Mersey, probably prior to her second maiden voyage on February 19, 1919, after reconditioning following First World War service, with the Royal Liver Building behind and the gleaming new Cunard Building on the right

LAST VOYAGE

Aquitania's final voyage nears its end, as she approaches the shipbreakers at Faslane, Scotland, exactly 31 years after the above photograph, on February 19, 1950

'I craved a warm fire'

CONTRACTED to design Aquitania's public spaces, Arthur Davis asked the Cunard directors: "Why don't you make a ship look like a ship?" and was told that "the people who use these ships are mostly seasick American ladies and the one thing they want to forget is that they are on a ship at all".

"Most of them have got to travel and they object to it very much. In order to impress that point upon me, the company sent me across the Atlantic," Davis said.

"The first day out I enjoyed the beautiful sea but when we got on well there was one thing I craved for as never before, and that was a warm fire and a pink shade.

"I suggest the transatlantic liner is not merely a ship, she is a floating town with three thousand passengers of all kinds and those who enjoy being there are distinctly in the minority.

"If we could get ships to look inside like ships and get people to enjoy the sea, it would be a very good thing – but all we can do, as things are, is to give them gigantic floating hotels."

UPPER CLASS
The A Deck landing of the First Class stairs

TOP AND BOTTOM
The smart four tall funnels and ventilation cowls contrast with the rudder and starboard inner propeller under repair in dry dock

INSTANT CLASSIC

Aquitania on February 19, 1919, at Princes Landing Stage, Liverpool, and ready for the off on her second maiden voyage to New York via Queenstown (Cobh), with all the bustle of people, trucks, carts and stores needed by this great ship

CASE STUDY

Above, passengers' luggage is loaded via an electric conveyor, while right, a seamen uses a bike on the liner's long boat deck

CROWD PULLER

People stroll along Gladstone Graving Dock in Bootle on May 14, 1914, to view the monster ship, with timber baulks being put in position to ensure she sits upright and on the centre line before the water is pumped out

MAIDEN VOYAGE

Aquitania at Princes Landing Stage prior to her maiden voyage to New York, on May 30, 1914, with an Isle of Man paddle steamer ahead and New Brighton Tower, top right. London boat trains would have arrived at Riverside Station, on the right, for the sailing

GREY LADY

World War Two and the black hull and white superstructure is gone after a repaint into troopship grey, although Aquitania's cowl vents and funnels still await disguise, as she lies alongside a Sydney shipyard in 1940. Note that a radar tower has been built ahead of the forward funnel

WALL OF STEEL

Workers leave Aquitania while she is overhauled at Southampton Floating Dry Dock, with her starboard anchor and chain neatly lowered for inspection

RULING THE SEA

Cunard's founder had a vision for scheduled, weekly transatlanic crossings with an emphasis on safety, but soon faced tough competition

THE sailing ship has been described as the most dangerous re-usable form of transport ever invented - but needs must and, as the modern world and international relations progressed ahead of technology, it relied on this elemental means to cross oceans.

The British government started North American mail packet sailings from Falmouth, Cornwall (being the UK's most westerly port), but these carried only a few officials and no cargo.

The harnessing of the steam engine for ship propulsion was the giant step forward and the American-owned PS Savannah was the first to achieve this feat partly by steam power in 1819 from Liverpool. Nearly 20 years later another paddle steamer, Sirius, achieved a crossing by steam only, taking 18 days, which was less then half of the average 40-day passage by sailing packet.

In 1839, the Canadian entrepreneur Samuel Cunard was awarded the lucrative first British transatlantic steamship Royal Mail contract as the only tender to guarantee a fortnightly service. The next year, with his partners, Cunard formed the British & North American Royal Mail Steam-Packet Co to operate the line's four pioneer paddle steamers on the Liverpool–Halifax–Boston route.

Samuel Cunard's vision – which became a reality – was a scheduled, weekly service with an emphasis on safety. Previously, transatlantic sailing ships completing a successful crossing could be weeks overdue.

Never complacent, within a few years Samuel Cunard became aware of Boston harbour's winter drawback of being ice-bound and moved his main western terminus further south to New York, where it remains to this day

Cunard's company dominated the transatlantic business for the next 30 years but by the 1870s was lagging behind its Liverpool-based rivals White Star Line and Inman Line. More capital was needed to meet this challenge, so the company was reorganised in 1879 as Cunard Steamship Co Ltd. White Star had practically invented the modern ocean liner with its Oceanic of 1870 and Teutonic of 1889.

Touring the latter at the Spithead Review caused Kaiser Wilhelm II to back the German bid for transatlantic supremacy and drive this international rivalry with the first passenger superliners. White Star Line, founded by Thomas Henry Ismay, was bought out in 1902 by US financier John Pierpoint Morgan's International Mercantile Marine Co in his bid to dominate transatlantic travel. Anxious that Cunard did not also succumb to join IMM, the British Government agreed to the company's request for big loans and a subsidy to build two new-style superliners to regain its competitive position.

The reinvigorated North German Lloyd and Hamburg America Line's new ocean greyhounds were also creaming off lucrative First Class passengers at Dover and Southampton.

Cunard's reply was the much-eulogised Mauretania of 1907 (holder of the Blue Riband of the Atlantic for the fastest crossing, 1909 to 1929) and her twin sister Lusitania.

With this new generation of the biggest and fastest speed queens, Cunard rose from looking like a sad also-ran to epitomise why Britannia ruled the waves.

But nothing is forever and in a ruthlessly competitive market, Cunard, when planning a third running mate to realise its three-ship weekly Liverpool - New York service, soon had to respond to what its deadly Mersey rival White Star was planning.

Cunard

EUROPE
AMERICA

Highway

BIG THREE

Cunard postcard of 1920s promoting, from left, Mauretania, Aquitania and Berengaria (ex-Imperator)

'Exceptional' ship

OCEAN liner historian Paul Louden-Brown believes the magnificence of the Aquitania is due, more than anything, to the idea that huge ships with amazing interiors were the way to go for express passenger liners in the early 1900s.

"Economy was the watchword and this policy, started by White Star Line, would have continued but for the First World War.

"White Star's chairman J Bruce Ismay was vilified for trying to break speed records with Titanic but that is wrong. What he was after was a reliable service," he said.

"Both Cunard and White Star wanted their services to be regarded as the 'ocean ferry', running with a reliability like a North Atlantic railway.

"This meant ships arrived at their destinations within a narrow time frame and onward travel arrangements could be depended upon.

"Aquitania was the zenith of the Edwardian luxury liner but after the First World War the social conditions she was built for were blown away.

"Yet she performed an unprecedented 30 years more of highly successful service which shows an astonishing adaptability for a ship of her great size.

"Like her White Star rival Olympic, she was the training ground for the most talented skippers who would rise to commodore level on the two original Cunard Queens.

"During wartime she was driven very hard and no doubt maintenance was less than in peacetime, yet she gave exceptional service, almost matching the Queens in her contribution to the Allied war effort, moving vast amounts of men and equipment. She was a war-winning weapon and doubtless near the top of the German Nazi hit-list.

"She encompassed four factors: economy, reliability, longevity and popularity. Her record is unmatched in the historic narrative of the North Atlantic."

SHEER BEAUTY

Aquitania shows her derriere to fine effect at Southampton, in 1921

Cunard Line
R.M.S. "Aquitania."

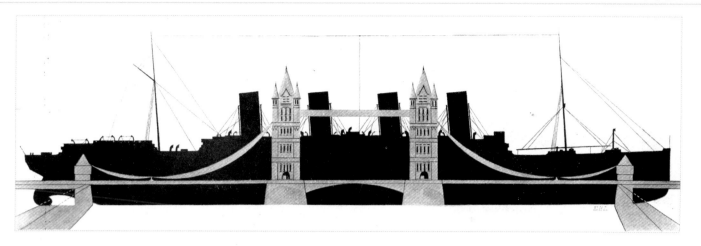

TOWERING

Shipping lines loved showing the huge size of their vessels compared to landmark buildings, here Aquitania sizes up to London's Tower Bridge

DIRTY WORK

In contrast to the liner's First Class splendours were the awful conditions for the engine room 'black gang' when still coal-fired. These firemen worked in the ship's bowels, stoking the boilers way beneath the funnels indicated by the black cylinders in the cross-section below

A LEGEND IS BORN

More than 100,000 people turned up to see Aquitania's big launch, an event that was deemed so important a public holiday was declared

Such was the drama and excitement associated with the launching of Aquitania, following 10 months of construction on Clydebank, that Glasgow Corporation declared a public holiday on April 21, 1913, so everyone who desired could view the first movement of the largest ship ever built there.

More than 100,000 spectators crammed into the shipyard and on the riverbanks around John Brown's shipyard for this once-only event.

In an appropriate choice for Merseyside, Countess Alice, wife of the 17th Earl of Derby (and Lord Mayor of Liverpool), stood on the launch platform and at 12.30pm christened Aquitania by pressing the button which swung the champagne bottle to smash on the bow and, more importantly, to release the hydraulic triggers that held the great ship immobile on the ways, after all other props were removed.

But nothing happened. As the seconds ticked away, then one, two and three minutes passed, no doubt the launch party must have stood as frozen in shock as the mammoth hull appeared to be stuck.

Yet to the multitude on the ground below there was an entirely different atmosphere. Sounds of creaking and cracking wooden ➤

STACKING

The third of Aquitania's four funnels is lifted into place at John Brown & Co's Clydebank fitting-out basin, in 1913

NEW HORIZON

Aquitania seen in a Cunard poster, circa 1920

CUNARD

baulks grew louder as the law of gravity asserted itself and the ship's timber cradle lost grip on the ways covered with tallow, oil and soap.

Then the vessel herself, as if waking from an embryonic unconsciousness, started imperceptibly to move, gathering speed to ten feet per second with a thunderous roar of her drag chains and entered her natural element one minute and 31 seconds later.

It might have been assumed that Aquitania's building contract would go to the Tyneside's shipyard of Swan Hunter & Wigham Richardson, which provided Cunard Line with its record-breaking speed queen Mauretania of 1907.

Instead, it was awarded on December 10, 1910, to John Brown & Co, Clydebank, Scotland, builders of Mauretania's sistership Lusitania, with whom Cunard had a strong relationship.

Aquitania's keel was laid on June 11, 1911, at Yard Number 409, on the same slipway as Lusitania was constructed five years earlier.

But with Aquitania some 50 per cent larger at 45,647 gross tons compared to Lusitania's 31,550 gross tons, the slipway had to be enlarged and strengthened, and the River Clyde and fitting out basin dredged to take her great size.

Naval architect Leonard Peskett obviously based her enlarged design on his previous Cunard twins Lusitania and Mauretania, giving Aquitania four funnels.

Her superstructure was a deck higher and closely resemble Peskett's smaller two-funnelled Cunard sister ships Carmania and Caronia. Overall, Aquitania had a boxier and more business-like look than the sheer elegance of her direct rivals, the White

Star Line's Olympic class, built at Harland & Wolff, Belfast, but this was offset by the elegant nine-degree rake of her funnels and masts.

Financed entirely by Cunard with no Government help (unlike Lusitania and Mauretania), Aquitania still met Admiralty requirements for war service as an armed merchant cruiser and her decks were strengthened for gun mounts. While still on the stocks, Aquitania was briefly the largest ship in the world until the building of the Germany's 52,226 gross ton Imperator.

Modifications were incorporated during fitting out from lessons learned from the Titanic disaster of just a year earlier.

Not least was Aquitania being one of the first ships to carry enough lifeboats for everybody onboard, with two of them motorized launches equipped with Marconi wireless.

Once again, thousands lined the banks of the Clyde on May 10, 1914, to see Aquitania's first tentative move under her own steam power from Brown's fitting-out basin to the Tail O' the Bank, Greenock, in the Firth of Clyde, where she was fully coaled and ballasted.

Two days later, her builders' trials over the traditional Arran Mile run in the Firth showed off her paces by steaming effortlessly at 24 knots, a full knot faster than her agreed service speed. Once trials were completed, she sailed south for Liverpool and entered the new Gladstone Graving Dock for hull cleaning and painting.

DARE TO DREAM

Naval architect Leonard Peskett

> ## "While still on the stocks, Aquitania was briefly the largest ship in the world"

FINALLY AFLOAT
Minutes after launching, on April 21, 1913, Aquitania is manouevred into her fitting-out berth

CUNARD LINER 'AQUITANIA' LEAVING WAYS – ENTERING WATER

WAVE OF EXPECTATION
Left, prior to launch, Aquitania's bow rears over the shipyard. Above, thousands lined the banks of the Clyde to watch the launch

TESTING TIME

Aquitania acquits herself on the Arran Mile, Firth of Clyde, during her builders' speed trials on May 12, 1914

"She came out of the mist in her great bulk, passed by the crowds gathered at each vantage point and receded again in impressive, stately silence."

Capt E Diggle on Aquitania's first sailing from her Clydebank builders

CITY AT SEA

A cross section of the liner showing how the different services, spaces and classes fitted together

FIRST ENTRANCE

Aquitania is gingerly edged into the Gladstone Graving Dock for hull inspection, cleaning and painting after arrival from her Clyde trials on May 14, 1914. Below, the incredible bulk of Aquitania's streamlined hull dwarfs the men inspecting the port inner propeller

GRACEFUL

The exquisite curves of Aquitania's counter stern and tapered hull together render her more akin to a racing yacht than a huge liner, as she sits at Gladstone Graving Dock

BRUSHING UP

Above, Gladstone Graving Dock workers clean more than 12 months' marine growth off the liner's hull before her maiden voyage. Left, an awestruck worker gazes at her rudder and starboard inner propeller. Below, around 100 John Brown shipyard workers had to sail on the maiden voyage to finish the last details, as seen here on the Promenade Deck

AMERICA CALLING

Aquitania's maiden voyage should have been a huge celebration but it was overshadowed by the sinking of RMS Empress of Ireland the previous day, a tragedy which cost the lives of more than 1,000 people

ON the morning of Aquitania's maiden voyage to New York on May 30, 1914, American newspaper, The Journal of Commerce wrote: "In the public mind, as well as among shipowners, the keenest interest has prevailed for some time in regard to the special features of the Cunard quadruple screw Royal mail steamer Aquitania, which is Britain's largest liner.

"It has been known in well-informed circles that from the conception of the vessel's designs, careful and masterly attention was conceived to introduce the highest standards of efficiency from two points of view – the power, the stability and speed of the vessel, and secondly, the domestic arrangements to meet the requirements of the most fastidious travellers.

"The first public inspection occurred yesterday, when by the courtesy of the directors of the Cunard Line nearly 1,000 guests visited the ship, these being principal Passenger Agents, Railway Representatives, and representatives of the principal newspapers of Great Britain. The guests boarded the great ➤

MOVING ON

Dressed overall, Aquitania steams slowly astern out of Gladstone Graving Dock to prepare for her maiden voyage

POTENT SYMBOL

Even high and dry in Gladstone
Graving Dock, Aquitania's knife-like
prow exudes formidable power in
check, waiting to be unleashed to
slice through the Atlantic rollers

➤ liner while she lay in the Gladstone dock, and from the time they stepped on board in the forenoon to the time they left the vessel in the evening, they experienced a round of constant surprises as to the superb quality of the ship, and a round of princely hospitality at the hands of the owners.

"The chairman of the company, Mr A A Booth, escorted on board the Lord Mayor of Liverpool (Mr H R Rathbone) and the Lady Mayoress, who by their visit represented the intense civic interest which is taken throughout the city in this latest Cunard triumph.

"Shortly before one o'clock, the Aquitania was easily and gracefully taken out of the dock into the river, a proceeding which was witnessed by thousands of spectators, who lustily cheered her on the passage.

"In an age of wonderful ships, the Aquitania is the most wonderful of all, offering unrivalled facilities to the traveller, for her immense size affords wonderful scope in the direction of safety and comfort. The best of everything from men's minds and labour to material and method has been selected and utilised in the construction and equipment of this ship.

"The concentrated experience of the finest naval architects, the most brilliant engineering, together with the ripe knowledge of the comfort and requirements desired by the transatlantic passenger, are embodied in this latest Cunard mammoth.

"She will maintain, with the Lusitania and Mauretania, the Cunard Express Mail Service between Liverpool and New York. These two sister ships hold all Atlantic speed records, and with the Aquitania this express service will be unparalleled."

What should have been a well-deserved huge city celebration for the start of her maiden voyage on May 30, 1914, under Capt William Turner, of Wallasey, was in effect cancelled as a mark of respect to the horrific sinking of the Liverpool-bound RMS Empress of Ireland the day before.

The Canadian Pacific liner was rammed and sank with the loss of 1,012 souls. This was now a maritime city in mourning.

Aquitania completed just three round trips as a key part of Cunard's upgraded weekly Liverpool - Queenstown (Cobh) - New York express service before an even bigger cataclysmic event, which started far away from Liverpool when a relatively unknown Archduke Franz Ferdinand was assassinated in Sarajevo.

COMMANDER
Capt William Turner, of Wallasey, in full dress uniform. Aquitania's first master was later in command of Lusitania when she was sunk during the First World War

COMIC TURN
Comedian Harry Tate, who earlier performed at the ship's launch ceremony, with his wife, aboard Aquitania

MERSEY DEPARTURE

With New Brighton Tower in the mist over her bow, Aquitania's lovely profile is apparent as she heads downriver for New York on her maiden voyage

City in mourning after loss of Empress

THE story of the loss of the Empress of Ireland is every bit as tragic as the other two great Atlantic liners, Titanic and Lusitania.

All three vessels were lost within a few years of each other – Titanic,1912; Empress of Ireland, 1914; and Lusitania 1916.

Canadian Pacific's Empress Of Ireland was registered in Liverpool and ran between the city and Canada.

With 1,477 people on board, she sank in the early hours of May 29, 1914, shortly after leaving Quebec en route to Liverpool, following a fog-bound collision with the Norwegian vessel Storstad.

The Empress had plied the Liverpool-Quebec route from 1906 and nearly 100 transatlantic crossings were a successful tribute to her speed, reliability and comfort.

One of a fleet of Empress liners operated by the diversified CPR – Canadian

Pacific Railways – she was built on the Clyde and was the latest word in transatlantic luxury. None of this was now of any comfort to passengers and crew.

Among the 1,012 lost souls were 840 passengers, slightly higher than Titanic's 832 passengers and in excess of Lusitania's 791.

Around 90% of the ship's 420 crew came from Liverpool – the bulk of them from the Scotland Road area, which became a neighbourhood of widows and orphans.

The CPR offices at Liverpool's Liver Building was besieged by relatives – no fewer than 200 families were affected.

To mark the tragedy's exact centenary, a memorial service on May 29, 2014, was held at Our Lady & St Nicholas church, Liverpool, organised by the city's Merchant Navy Day committee.

"Aquitania combines
in one structure the
qualities of the most
modern hotel and the
speed almost of a gull"
Edward Keble Chatterton
Maritime journalist, 1914

LEAVING OF LIVERPOOL

Aquitania's graceful lines make a fabulous sight as she pulls away from Princes Landing Stage on her maiden voyage for Queenstown (Cobh) and New York, on May 30, 1914. In this superb panorama, crowds line the ship's rails and on the stage, where such is the clarity of detail you can see a babe in arms, bottom left (did papa survive the war to see his offspring grow up?)

DAILY

BELFAST
AND
LONDONDERRY
STEAMERS

PHOTOGRAPHS
R. M. S. AQUITANIA

International

AMBASSADOR HARVEY

...tographed with Mrs. Harvey on the
...deck of the "Aquitania," on which he
...ntly sailed to assume his duties as our
...bassador at the Court of St. James's, to
...ch position he was appointed by
President H...

CUNARD LINE

The Four-Screw Turbine Steamers
LUSITANIA and MAURETANIA, 32,000 Tons
ARE THE LARGEST FINEST AND FASTEST TURBINE VESSELS IN THE WORLD

ATLANTIC FLEET

AQUITANIA, — — Building
LACONIA, — — Twin-Screw, 18,000 Tons, Building

LIVERPOOL-NEW YORK SERVICE

CAMPANIA 12,950 Tons	LUSITANIA 32,000 Tons	
CARMANIA 20,000 Tons	MAURETANIA 32,000 Tons	
	CARONIA 20,000 Tons	

LIVERPOOL - BOSTON SERVICE

FRANCONIA 18,150 Tons

IVERNIA 14,210 Tons
FRANCONIA AND LACONIA, THE LARGEST STEAMERS IN THE
BOSTON SERVICE

CUNARD LINE
Liverpool, New York, Boston via Queenstown.

R.M.S. "AQUITANIA" QUADRUPLE SCREW, 47,000 TONS, LENGTH 901 FEET, BREADTH 97 FEET, DEPTH 92½ FEET.

MAIDEN ARRIVAL

Having passed the Statue of Liberty, in New York
harbour, the great liner nears her western terminus
for the first time, greeted by tugs and port, city
and Cunard officials in the white tender alongside.
Below, Aquitania's Palladian Lounge, based on a
saloon in Robert Adams' Lansdowne House, London

"In an age
of wonderful
ships, the
Aquitania
is the most
wonderful of
all, offering
unrivalled
facilities to
the traveller"

ALMOST THERE

Another view of Aquitania's New York debut,
showing how her high speed has rubbed off
the bow paint above the waterline

SMART

A First Class
suite, complete
with sash
windows
(no vulgar
portholes
here), floral
wallpaper,
wash basin and
electric fire

SUPERLINER TO SUPERTROOPER

After the start of the First World War, Aquitania was converted by the military into an armed merchant cruiser, trooper and hospital ship

Requisitioned by the government a mere three months after being completed as a luxury liner, Aquitania's finery was rapidly stripped out for conversion into a Royal Navy armed merchant cruiser and she left the Mersey four days later on her first week-long patrol in the Western Approaches.

This role lasted for an even shorter time than her previous civilian career, as on her second patrol the giant liner collided with her escort, the Leyland liner Canadian, in thick fog off Anglesey.

Once back in Liverpool, the Admiralty decided that Aquitania's great size made her unsuitable as an armed merchant cruiser.

Repaired in Liverpool by the end of 1914 and laid up there until May, 1915, Aquitania was then converted into a troopship for the Gallipoli Campaign, leaving Liverpool on June 15 with more than 5,000 troops.

After three round voyages carrying 30,000 troops to and from Dardanelles, she was converted into a hospital ship, sailing from December 1915 until January 1916. Aquitania was to return to Cunard service after being released from government service on April 10, 1916.

While being refurbished by Harland & Wolff at Southampton, the government requisitioned her again as a hospital ship in November 1916 until the end of the year, before lay-up in Liverpool for most of 1917.

DAZZLE SHIP

Sporting the dazzle scheme to confuse enemy attackers, Aquitania speeds along while a patrol boat struggles to keep up

SAFE HAVEN

Now in hospital ship livery, Aquitania anchored at
Mudros Bay, Lemnos, Greece, towers over her companion

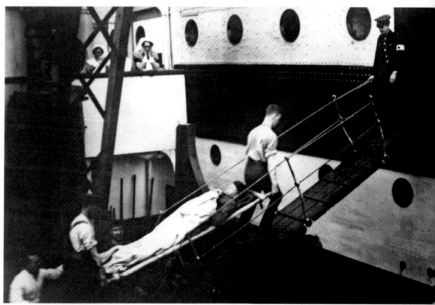

The US entered the war in April 1917
and, in December 1917, Aquitania was
reactivated for troopship duty. Repainted
in 'dazzle ship' livery – a design by artist
Norman Wilkinson to confuse the enemy
over a ship's size and direction – Aquitania
transported thousands of American and
Canadian troops, with 8,000 troops
onboard for one sailing.

She made her first calls at Halifax, Nova
Scotia, Canada, starting an association with
that city which would be rekindled in the
Second World War and after. In all, she
made nine transatlantic round voyages and
carried 60,000 US and Canadian troops
until the war ended in November 1918. It
was a tremendous achievement, not least
as she sailed in German U-boat and mine-
infested seas which claimed fellow British
superliners Lusitania and Britannic (II).

HOMEBOUND

Above, a wounded
soldier from
the Dardanelles
Campaign is
stretchered onto
Aquitania from the
smaller hospital
ship at Mudros,
watched by nurses

IN CHARGE

Left, Lt Col
F J Brown, Royal
Army Medical
Corps, and Capt C
A Smith on HMHS
Aquitania,
circa 1915

CRAZY PATTERN
Trooping in 'Dazzle Ship' livery

WARD ROOMS
Above, the Carolean Smoking Lounge on A Deck set up with beds ready to receive wounded officers, while just such a contingent fill the Palladian Lounge with medical staff, below

SEA AIR

Above, probably on a voyage home, medical staff and wounded soldiers cram onto the boat deck, itself chocker with extra lifeboats - with one already occupied by someone taking no chances

FLOATING HOSPITALS

Left, Aquitania at Mudros, with smaller hospital ship Essequibo, left, and another alongside

WHEN THE TWENTIES ROARED

After the war, Cunard invented a new market for tourism and Aquitania established herself as one of the most favoured and profitable luxury ocean liners in the world

WITH the First World War finally over and released from trooping duties, Aquitania made her first postwar peacetime voyage, departing from Liverpool on February 19, 1919, for Queenstown (Cobh) and New York.

Unfortunately for the city of her conception, she was thereafter based in Southampton during the '20s and '30s.

Cunard decided to follow its rival Liverpool company, White Star, in relocating its premier express transatlantic liners to the Hampshire port, with its deeper, wider, calmer waters and easier access to London and the continent.

While awaiting reconditioning, Aquitania ran an "austerity service" between Southampton and New York in June 1919.

Steaming to the Tyne in November 1919, she had a six month refit for post-war service at Armstrong Whitworth & Co.

Her original fittings were reinstalled, a gyro-compass fitted and she was converted from coal firing to oil, which reduced her engineroom crew - the 'black gang' - by 200 men at a stroke to just 140. Sadly a shipyard worker was killed by an explosion during the conversion.

Trials off northern Scotland were a

ALL THAT JAZZ

Right, a mid-Atlantic dance by well-dressed but rather stiff looking couples. Perhaps seasickness was kicking in? Below, an impromptu concert on deck by a touring US college band

success and on July 17, 1920 she restarted Cunard's express Southampton - Cherbourg - New York service. Once again she was part of a weekly three ship service, with her old running mate, the Blue Ribbon holder Mauretania and the newcomer Berengaria, formerly Hamburg America's Imperator, which was a war reparation for Germany's sinking of Lusitania.

Over the next decade, the 1920s did indeed roar for Aquitania, establishing herself as one of the most favoured and most profitable ocean liners. This was in spite of the US imposing immigration restrictions, initially by the 1917 Dillingham Act, which was revised and tightened in 1921 and 1924.

Although Aquitania and her like had the public image of being luxury liners, much of their earnings were based on carrying large numbers of immigrants and suddenly this lucrative trade evaporated. In a decade westbound immigrants fell from one million in 1913 to 150,000 in 1923.

All credit to Cunard and its rivals for adapting so smartly and inventing a new market for tourism, guided groups and student travellers to fill their berths.

Meantime, on the upper decks paraded the celebrity passengers of royalty, aristocracy, politicians and the growing numbers of film stars, which steamship lines loved to publicise. ➤

➤ Fashionable photographer and designer Cecil Beaton dismissed a voyage on her as "back on the boring old Aquitania again", but such a socialite would not have been aboard anything but the best.

Passenger capacity was as high as any modern cruise liner. During the mid-1920s, Aquitania could carry 2,000 people with 610 first class, 950 second class and 640 tourist class. She wasn't only sustained by her Ship Beautiful reputation, but by providing the best service at sea.

Maritime author John Malcolm Brinnin wrote: "Aquitania had the advantage of a crew trained in a sort of father-to-son heritage of stewardship that marked whole families in Liverpool and Southampton to give service on a scale of British tact, grace and professionalism that positively dizzied American travellers."

To meet these changes Cunard invested in modernising Aquitania in her annual winter refits of 1926, 1927 and 1928. Another innovation was her use as a floating art gallery for a voyage in 1930.

Intriguingly, while Aquitania's first class public rooms received much acclaim it was her pared-down third class accommodation, with its exposed bulkheads and rivetted frames and ribs that impressed upon a young Swiss architect. That minimalist style, stripped of decoration deeply influenced Le Corbusier, whose mantra of "function is beauty" has had a massive impact on international postwar urban planning and design. Unwittingly, this is arguably Aquitania's greatest legacy. Altogether the future looked bright with fair weather and following seas, but over the horizon there was an almighty crash ahead.

Not a collision of the iceberg variety that doomed Titanic, but a more far-reaching economic catastrophe – the Wall Street Crash of October 1929 and the Great Depression that followed.

OIL'S WELL

Aquitania revs up after conversion to oil burning at Armstrong Whitworth's Naval Shipyard, River Tyne, in April, 1920

Food, glorious food

A LIFE of luxury has been on the menu for Cunard passengers for decades, but some of the whims often presented a big challenge to the chefs.

An American oil magnate on the Aquitania once asked for a rattlesnake steak for four. His order was gravely accepted and he was served with eels in a silver salver, borne by two stewards shaking rattles, and followed by a serious-faced chef in a two-foot high hat.

Jewish passengers had their own butcher and kitchen, to ensure kosher meat and cooking, and notices posted up about hours of meals, regulations and so on, were printed in half a dozen languages.

A menu from 1921 offers third-class passengers a lunch of tomato and bean soup; roast beef with brown gravy, dressed cabbage and boiled potatoes; and plum pudding with sweet sauce.

Meanwhile, the first-class bill of fare includes paprika shrimps, Bordeaux sardines, lambs' tongues, grilled fillets of haddock, smoked sausage and sour cabbage, stuffed shoulder of lamb, as well as a cold buffet of roast beef, Cumberland ham, ox tongue, boar's head and galantine of veal.

WHAT'S COOKING

Top, some of the meat, game and poultry used for a Christmas voyage. Above, crew at work in the kosher kitchen

RECIPE FOR SUCCESS

After enjoying a meal in the First Class Elizabethan Grill (above) passengers may have burned off some calories in the pillared swimming pool or gymnasium (below)

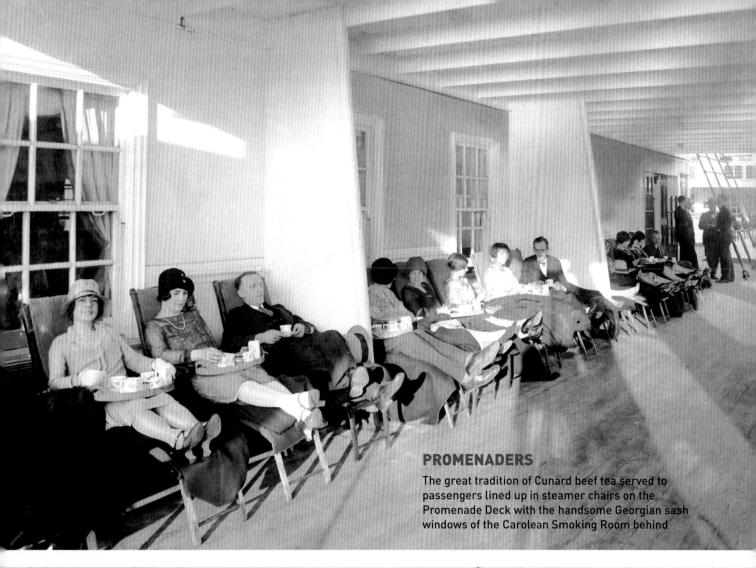

PROMENADERS

The great tradition of Cunard beef tea served to passengers lined up in steamer chairs on the Promenade Deck with the handsome Georgian sash windows of the Carolean Smoking Room behind

LUXURY LINER

"For the rich and titled, Aquitania catered beautifully. Her accommodations in first class were especially dream-like, a fantasy world gone to sea..."
William H Miller Jnr,
Ocean Liner Chronicles

The Romance of a Modern Liner

THIS was the highly readable memoir of one of Aquitania's famous masters, Capt EG Diggle RD RNR, providing the definitive description of the great ship up until the late 1930s and lavishly illustrated.

ROUND ONE

Above, a boxing match gets plenty of interest from crew and passengers on the aft Boat Deck. Below, for the more delicate there was the 'biscuit and whistle' relay race - clearly no less fun

NATURAL GROWTH

Flowers are stocked for the Garden Lounges located on either side of the ship

GULL'S EYE VIEW

Right, looking aft from the foremast crow's nest, with the forward funnel and giant cowl vents looming over the officers

THRILLS AND DRILLS

Left, the Boat Deck is host to table tennis matches with afternoon tea, and below, officers explaining lifeboat drills to belted passengers

"The North Atlantic – the big and fast steamer route – is fixed in the popular imagination by a succession of notable, historic, and, romantic events. It is the Atlantic Ferry which is invested with the greatest romance in the mind of thousands of people, the majority of whom have never crossed the ocean in their lives."

CHOCKS AWAY

Preparing to lower a lifeboat

KEPT IN LINE

The bell boys about to start their morning "physical jerks"

SWEET TOOTH

Taking the first bite of a sugar model of Aquitania (with Cunard's first vessel Britannia in front) made by the ship's confectioner

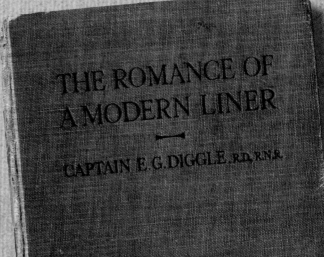

THE ROMANCE OF A MODERN LINER

CAPTAIN E. G. DIGGLE, R.D. R.N.R.

ATTENTION WINNER

With spectators even clinging onto a railway van, the crowds gawp at Southampton for a glimpse of the Epsom Derby winner Papyrus, being led onto Aquitania to sail to New York in 1922, for an unsuccessful race against the Kentucky Derby winner Zev. This was international news as Papyrus was the first British horse sent to the US for a single race. He enjoyed his own custom-built stable and staff

TALLY HO!

British fox hounds look keen for their trip to take part in a US hunt

DRIVING FORCE

Like the great lady she was, Aquitania points her prow into the English Channel breakers and seemingly unperturbed ploughs on westwards to New York

The wonders of the wonder ship

"THIS is the Rolls-Royce of the seas," remarked Viscount Northcliffe, while touring Aquitania's engine room. "You mean Rolls-Royce is the Aquitania of the road!" replied her chief engineer George Patterson

"They call this Aquitania the Wonder Ship of the World and I think they are perfectly right," Northcliffe wrote in a Daily Mail review in the 1920s.

"Nowhere in the world, whether it be in the last word in swift luxurious ships or the latest American hotels, will you find such comfort, such luxury, such amazing, scrupulous cleanliness in every smallest detail, all produced by that genie, Perfect Organisation."

"From the Games Deck to the Cheese Deck, about 10 decks down, where the Stiltons ripen in dark places and reverend wines grow to a yet greater perfection, there are only three smells - sea, flowers and soap. The keenest nose in the world would never sniff 'ship'."

"The Long Gallery: remember the long hall into which Alice in Wonderland fell out of the well - low, long, with hanging lamps and doors on each side? This is Aquitania's Alice Gallery, and that nothing may be missing, a children's nursery lies below, crammed with toys."

"Aquitania is not a 'floating hotel', any more than a good yacht is a 'floating flat'.

"Hotels and flats are full of noise and restlessness and are generally overcrowded. The Wonder Ship is a glorious country house with just the right number of people and plenty of room for them all."

"I have only one complaint to offer Aquitania's owners.

"She averages over 22 knots and I can only spend a week at a time aboard her, because she gets there too soon."

PRECIOUS CARGO

Above, mountains of mail bags sent down chutes from Aquitania ready to be landed by tender probably at Cherbourg or Queenstown (Cobh). Right, silver bars are unloaded in what appears to be fairly relaxed security

ALL IN A DAY

Top, stewards take dirty linen ashore for the laundry. Left, a packed New York pier as Aquitania backs into the River Hudson to start another voyage. Above, the ship's wheel, gyroscopic repeater and magnetic compass

CRUISES FOR ALL

A drop in transatlantic passengers and the US Prohibition on alcohol, heralded the era of the 'booze cruise'

EVEN after a quarter century of service Aquitania still held her status as one of the world's premier liners.

This is perfectly illustrated by her namecheck in Alfred Hitchcock's film 1939 film Rebecca, in which American socialite Mrs Van Hopper impetuously decides to return from the French Riviera to New York and demands that her young companion "makes reservations on the Aquitania immediately".

However, maintaining this lofty position at the top of the Merchant Navy tree had been a long and lumpy passage for Aquitania and her rivals, most of which fell by the wayside.

Following the Wall Street Crash of 1929, the Great Depression caused dramatic drop in passenger and freight leading to a slump in shipping. By 1932, transatlantic passenger numbers fell to 600,000 annually, which was less than a quarter of their two and a half million peak in 1913. ➤

CUNARD QUARTET

Packed into Ocean Dock, Southampton, on March 28, 1930, are the Cunard liners, from left, Aquitania, Mauretania, Ausonia and Laconia. The latter was one of the worst wartime merchant disasters in 1942, with 1,649 people lost

"From New York, Aquitania and her fellow express liners roamed up and down the eastern US and Canadian seaboards"

➤ Wealthy travellers faded away and the immigrant trade was a distant memory.

To keep costly ships and crews occupied, Cunard and other lines turned to cruising and at least for this they were aided by the US Prohibition on alcohol.

Thirsty Americans who would not normally have considered a holiday afloat found the notion of an inexpensive, long weekend voyage very enticing.

Thus was born the "booze cruise". From New York, Aquitania and her fellow express liners roamed up and down the eastern US and Canadian seaboards, either on "cruises to nowhere" (but with the bars open throughout), or on short hops to Cuba and Bermuda. Costing about $10 a day, most of these passengers probably had never sailed before on a liner.

Aquitania's first cruise on February 3, 1932, was an ambitious eight week round trip from New York to the eastern Mediterranean. Its hot climate destinations were far from what her designers had planned for a "indoor" ship on the cold windswept North Atlantic, yet it was popular enough for her to repeat the itinerary several times.

There was also the chance to sail on a six day Southampton-Gibraltar round cruise for a mere £5.

In November of that year the liner had another refurbishment, with first class berths reduced to 650, tourist class expanded to 600 berths and third class now at 900 capacity. A theatre and cinema was fitted and the public spaces refreshed.

In 1934, courtesy of the Depression, two of Aquitania's fleetmates - Mauretania and

PARTY TIME
Revellers during a fancy
dress night on a 1930s cruise

Olympic - in the newly combined Cunard White Star Line fleet were sold for scrap, leaving her as the last pre-First World War four funnelled express liner.

Also in 1934 and 1938, the company disposed of Majestic and Berengaria which both started life for the rival German transatlantic Hamburg America Line before being ceded to the UK as war reparations for the loss of Britannic (II) and Lusitania.

What stands out is Aquitania's reliability, which kept her out of the headlines as staying on schedule isn't news.

However on April 10, 1935, the press made the most of her grounding in the Solent on Thorne Knoll, near Southampton, during which she had to wait for the next high tide to be refloated, giving amble opportunity for aerial photographs of 10 tug boats straining to free her.

By now rapidly advancing marine technology was also forcing the older liner generation's disposal.

Germany was recovering with two new record-breaking superliners Europa and Bremen, the latter taking the Blue Ribbon of the Atlantic from Mauretania, which had held it for 22 years.

With British government help, Cunard White Star got finance to complete Britain's biggest superliner RMS Queen Mary (I),

which entered service amid much hullabaloo in 1936.

Imitation is the best form of flattery and Queen Mary was very much an enlarged, modernised version of Aquitania and just as successful.

Interestingly, with a depleted Cunard fleet and as the line waited for QM's new running mate, Queen Elizabeth (I) to be launched in September 1938, Aquitania's sailing schedule was intensified while her replacement was readied to enter service in 1940. In spite of being the "slow coach" of Cunard's original express trio, the now 24-years-old Aquitania was being pushed to average 24.87 knots a voyage, nearly two knots faster than her planned service speed of 23 knots.

There was still time for cruises and in February 1938 Aquitania made another unusual voyage from New York, this time to the Carnival in Rio de Janeiro, Brazil.

She was in the company of two great new ships of state, French Line's flagship SS Normandie and Italian Line's flagship SS Rex, both of which were recent former Blue Ribbon holders.

Anchored off Rio alongside these sleek, modern speed queens Aquitania must have looked to all as the stately old maiden aunt, sitting it out alongside the glamorous new generation. Yet paradoxically, the forthcoming war which was to destroy these two magnificent modern liners was to be Aquitania's saving grace. Echoing Mark Twain's famous riposte on seeing his own obituary published, news of her demise was premature.

And on another filmic note, Aquitania is seen in the 1940 comedy The Road to Singapore coming to the rescue of Bob Hope, adrift on a life raft. Aquitania in the South China Sea?! Presumably what was simply Hollywood stock footage of a big ship in fact turned out to be an uncannily accurate prophecy in this amazing liner's next career chapter.

HIGH NOTE

Top, a crew member runs a well-patronised 'horse race' event on board a cruise. Above, the more sedate pleasure of listening to a fellow passenger tickle the ivories

PASSING TRADE

Passengers watch a British India cargo liner from Aquitania's rails, possibly during one of her £5 return cruises to Gibraltar. Below, even Cunard's heraldic lions were used to promote the fun of cruising in cartoon form

R.M.S.
Aquitania
Berengaria
Mauretania

Cunard
Express Service

"Thirsty Americans, who would not normally have considered a holiday afloat, found the notion of an inexpensive, long weekend voyage very enticing"

"THREE JOLLY SAILORS"

R.O. Longmire

ONBOARD DRAMA

Above, a crew show in the new theatre-cinema installed in 1932. Left, a twin berth First Class stateroom after one of the 1930s refits

ALL IN FUN

Below, a fancy dress party pose on the boat deck, including costumes of the Stars and Stripes and Union Jack

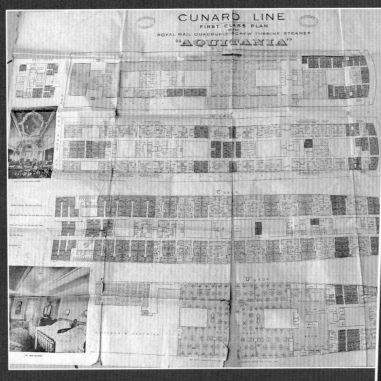

The mysterious Frank Owen

WHO were the now anonymous 30,000 passengers who filled Aquitania's staterooms and cabins each year, creating the very need for her existence?

One such individual was Frank Owen, aged 27, who grew up in very humble circumstances in Wem, Shropshire, the son of a machinist and quarryman, but later travelled First Class, all expenses paid on Aquitania.

Keen to get out and get on, Frank Owen emigrated to Quebec, Canada, on the Canadian Pacific liner Montrose, to become a farmer, on May 18, 1926.

His great nephew Stephen Done, of New Brighton, who is a detective novelist, said: "We don't know what happened, but he next turns up in South America's oil industry, becoming a highly successful 'petrolero', to-ing and fro-ing across the Atlantic in First Class on company business.

"We have the Montrose passenger list for his outbound trip and also an Aquitania list for a westbound voyage on January 4, 1933, from Southampton to New York, which states his "country of intended future residence is Colombo, South America".

"On arrival in New York he presumably transferred to a banana boat for the second leg to South America. We've a splendid First Class deck plan indicating his inside cabin and the public rooms, as given to passengers.

"He married a lady called Peggy Dwyer, who was New York's first lady taxi, and they later lived in great luxury in Vancouver, Canada. Frank was persuaded out of retirement to be boss of the famous oil well trouble shooter Red Adair. However, they lost their only son, a pilot, who was killed when his crop dusting plane crashed into power cables, and the light went out of their lives."

FAMILY HISTORY

Stephen Done with the deck plans for the Aquitania, which carried his great uncle Frank Owen from Southampton to New York in 1933

DRYING OUT

Aquitania enters Southampton Dry Dock for her 1932 refit

TOP DRAWER

Not merely pastiche, Aquitania's interiors were celebrated thanks to designer Arthur Davis' talent and John Brown's Clydebank skilled craftsmen working with the finest material unobtainable today

PROPPED UP

Above, two shipyard workers take a break on one of the liner's new propellers before fitting, when it will later turn at around 160 revolutions per minute. Right, other workers dangle precariously repainting the superstructure

WELL VENTILATED

The highly exposed open upper bridge which was later enclosed with an upper wheelhouse

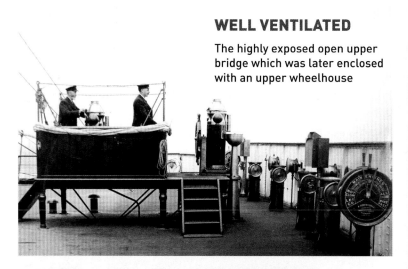

CHAIN GANG

The liners high sides are seen in Southampton Dry Dock in 1932, and above, shipyard workers check the anchor chain links on the foredeck

Transatlantic style

POET and critic John Malcolm Brinnin in 'Grand Luxe - The Transatlantic Style', wrote: "A dowager and the last of her kind, Aquitania maintained an aristocratic presence on the sea-lanes long after bigger and more powerful ships had come and gone, long after airy suites taking their decorative schemes form Gainsborough and Constable were but footnotes to lost graciousness.

"Then staterooms on the Atlantic would feature all the push-button convenience of an airport hotel, along with dining rooms as bare and banal as commissaries.

"Given the chance, who would not turn a corner and, in the warp of time, step onto the royal-blue carpeting of Aquitania's restaurant, claim a white table glinting with silver and crystal and study a menu in its two deck high well of sunlight at lunch and its hundred circles of lamp-light at dinner?"

BACK IN BATTLE

Just as the end seemed nigh and Aquitania faced being withdrawn from service, she found herself needed for wartime duty once again

THERE was general agreement that with the arrival of RMS Queen Elizabeth in 1940, Aquitania would be withdrawn, as at long last Cunard had two liners big enough to run a weekly transatlantic service between them.

But with war breaking out in September 1939, history repeated itself and what was the end for so much was a reprieve for Aquitania. Not that survival was a certainty.

Having dashed back from New York to Southampton, she made a final civilian voyage, especially for Americans wanting to leave Europe quickly. Mindful of the Lusitania disaster, passengers attended a meeting onboard warning them that travel was at their own risk. News was already spreading of SS Athenia's sinking by a U-boat outbound from Liverpool (the first merchant ship attacked in the war) and many US passengers disembarked.

To confuse U-boats, Aquitania missed out her Cherbourgh call and sped across to New York. Once again she was requisitioned as a troop transport, from November 21, 1939.

She was converted to carry 7,724 servicemen and initially assigned to transport Canadian troops.

In 1940, Aquitania underwent a refit in the United States and was defensively armed with six-inch guns.

She stayed docked in New York waiting for further orders. Queen Elizabeth made her secret maiden crossing across the Atlantic and met up with Aquitania in New York where, together with Queen Mary and Normandie, the four ships made an unforgettable sight.

In March, Aquitania sailed for Sydney, Australia, in her Cunard livery, for the further transport of Australian and New Zealand troops. She made two passages

between Pearl Harbor and San Francisco.

Later in 1940, Aquitania took part in what was dubbed the millionaire ship convoy, sailing out of Sydney with Queen Mary, Queen Elizabeth, Queen of Bermuda, Nieuw Amsterdam and Ile de France.

Now in battleship grey, Aquitania was in Singapore in November 1941.

Allegedly, the crew of the German auxiliary raider Kormoran heard of Aquitania's departure from Singapore and planned to ambush her, but encountered the Australian cruiser HMAS Sydney instead on November 19. After a mutually destructive battle, both ships sank.

Aquitania arrived on the scene and picked up the survivors of Kormoran, the Aquitania's captain going against orders not to stop for survivors. There were no survivors from HMAS Sydney.

Aquitania served eight years in wartime trooping service, latterly on Atlantic runs.

She steamed more than 500,000 miles and carried nearly 400,000 soldiers and other military staff all over the world in a guise and in climates far from her preconceived role as a queen of the North Atlantic.

THE LONG GOODBYE

Aquitania in the Straits of Gibraltar after bringing sailors to reinforce the Royal Navy's Mediterranean fleet there in 1940. Did this smartly dressed lady have a loved one onboard?

CAPE ARRIVAL

Aquitania steams into Table Bay – with Table Mountain in the mist behind –
for a call at Cape Town, South Africa, from New York in 1940

DEEP SOUTH

Arriving where it was never anticipated she would sail, Aquitania acquaints herself with the
Sydney Harbour Bridge, Australia, prior to full conversion into a troopship in 1940

'Can you keep up?'

IN his book Liners To The Sun, maritime historian John Maxtone-Graham recounts a tale from Aquitania's first crossing back to England in the Second World War, by which time Aquitania was the only four-funnelled liner still in existence.

During this crossing, an old destroyer from the reserves came out to meet her and signalled with an Aldis lamp, "FOUR FUNNEL SHIP PLEASE INDICATE."

Captain George Gibbon's reply was, "We are the only ******** four-funnel ship in the world and that so-and-so wants our name. Tell him to read 'The News of the World.'"

The destroyer signaled again, asking, "DO YOU REQUIRE AN ESCORT"?

Aquitania, meant to run in tandem with Lusitania and Mauretania, the fastest ships on the Atlantic, signalled back, "CAN YOU KEEP UP?"

Aquitania continuing at full speed, began to outdistance the destroyer. The final signal from the other destroyer read, "YOUR FINE SPEED REQUIRES LITTLE PROTECTION."

"Aquitania was sure elusive and changed course every nineteen minutes, because it took 20 minutes for a German submarine to get through the complicated process of firing its torpedo. It must have taken us ten days for a five-day crossing, as we went twice as far in a zig-zag"

US GI Robert Towle on 1943 voyage to Scotland

WAR HORSE

Wearied by six years of war, Aquitania has at least regained her red and black Cunard funnel livery but is still in troopship mode. The lifeboats still hang over the side for speedy evacuation and to allow extra ones to be packed onto the boat deck to serve the far greater number of people onboard

"I was in F deck, which I believe was the lowest level. We did the zig-zag as I was in the stern of the ship and at night I could hear the clanging of the rudder chain as they changed course every 20 minutes."
Peder Perdsen,
ex-Royal Canadian Air Force, 1943

Evacuation of Honolulu

"IN April 1942, my mother, my sisters and I travelled on Aquitania from Honolulu to San Francisco. We were hundreds of military dependents being transported out of the war zone after the attack on Pearl Harbor.

"While at sea we were fired upon by a Japanese sub that had only two charges left. The watch could see the torpedoes go behind the stern.

"The rumour was that 'the cook' threw potato peelings overboard, thus drawing the sub's attention. The radio operator picked up the message from the sub reporting us sunk.

"Aquitania's speed surely had a great deal to do with the torpedo miss and also we were in a stormy seas for most of the trip. We were travelling with SS Lurline, of Matson Line. Lurline would go down in a trough and

we could barely see her stacks (funnels). She would rise on the crest and we would slide down.

" When we arrived at San Francisco Bay, the ship had to sit outside and wait for the tide to go out, as she was too tall to clear the Golden Gate Bridge at high tide."

**Jeannette Atkins
Pearl Harbor survivor
(then aged seven years)**

ATLANTIC TRANSPORTS

Two of the three largest troopships in the Second World War in the Clyde during May 1942, with the newly-arrived Queen Mary about to disgorge North American military into a flotilla of small ships at her side, while the unmistakable silhouette of Aquitania is steaming away on the right

END OF AN ERA

The war ended but Aquitania steamed on, as busy as ever. But by now, she was living on borrowed time and time was taking its toll on the old lady

The Ship Beautiful had become Old Irrepressible. One wonders what a help it would have been to the Allied cause if her contemporaries such as Berengaria, Olympic and Majestic had not been prematurely withdrawn and scrapped because of the Depression.

A year after hostilities ceased, Aquitania was still shuttling back and forth across the Atlantic, repatriating Canadian and American troops, continuing her association with Halifax, NS, which had started in the previous World War. With trooping duties finally over after three postwar years, Cunard Line finally had its ship returned by the Ministry of Transport on April 1, 1948.

In a new lease of life, she was chartered by the Canadian Government to carry the wives and children of Canadian servicemen over to Canada, with Halifax again her western terminus. Canada renewed the contract in 1949 until December 1.

Samuel Cunard's home town, Halifax, remains proud of this association and its Maritime Museum of the Atlantic has the ship's wheel and a large builder's model on display. ➤

PEACE AT LAST

In the immediate aftermath of war and amid quayside activity, an apparently deserted Aquitania slumbers at her Southampton berth, right, with a vestige of normality reappearing, with repainted white foremast, derricks and cowl vents, while Queen Mary is manouevred, left. Both liners have at least regained their Cunard funnel liveries

➤ During this period, Cunard staff based at its Liverpool Pier Head headquarters, recall arriving for work one misty morning and seeing the great four stacker lying at Princes Landing Stage, even by then "looking like something from another lost age".

By now the Aquitania was living on borrowed time and she was not granted an operating license for 1950.

Three and a half decades of almost non-stop service is a very long time in ship years and time was taking its toll on the old lady.

Her decks leaked in wet weather and the rot set in to such an extent that according to Cunard commodore Harry Grattidge in his 'Captains of the Queens' memoir, it became so bad a piano had fallen through the deck above into a corporate luncheon.

At the same time, Cunard had finally realised its 1930s ambition of reducing its three ship weekly transatlantic service to a two-ship one, which was achievable with the original Queen Mary and Queen Elizabeth, so rebuilding Aquitania was both too costly and unnecessary.

As it was, the 1939 Birkenhead built Mauretania (II) was already on hand as a standby for the Queens. Time was finally called on January 9, 1950, when Hampton's auctioned Aquitania's furnishings and Cunard sold her later that month to the British Iron & Steel Corp for £125,000.

Slipping quietly out of Southampton, Aquitania steamed to Faslane, Scotland for scrapping.

A vessel of truly remarkable character had left the centre stage of Britain's mercantile marine after 36 years.

PULLING POWER

Two Alexandra tugs belch smoke while docking troopship Aquitania

END IS NIGH

Aquitania, lying at Berth 108, Southampton's 'Death Row', as her nemesis finally arrives in the form of Queen Elizabeth, right, with Mauretania (II) behind, early in 1950

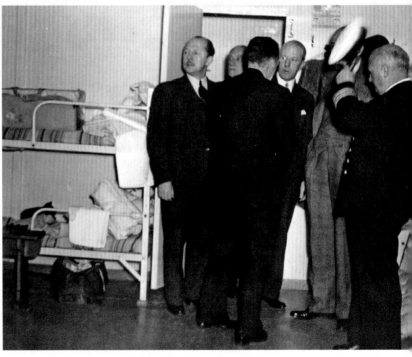

GUIDED TOUR

The Canadian High Commissioner and officials view the liner prior to her immigrant voyage charter

Emotional wait for our war brides

By Olive Owens

"I HAD not seen my Canadian husband since August 1944 and it was March 1946. My first sight of the Aquatania and I was full of wonder and apprehension.

"I had never seen an ocean liner before, she looked magnificent!

"Inside the ship was gutted as she had been used for carrying service men. There were rows of bunks three high. Quite a few of the girls were sea sick even before we left Southampton.

"As we left the dock a brass band played Auld Lang Syne and I don't think there was a dry eye on board. Our first meal was wonderful - steak! We hadn't seen steak for years. The girls with children and expectant mothers were separated from those of us who didn't have children.

"Two days into our journey we hit a dreadful storm, the portholes were blocked but the water still came through. The water was up to my mattress on my bunk and my clothes were soaking wet. I was extremely sick as were the two girls above me. As well as being wet I was also covered in vomit. Most of the crew and nursing staff were ill. They had to stop the engines to perform an appendicitis and three babies were born. To go to the washroom you were ankle deep at least in water.

"Apparently they also lost radio contact for a while. Eventually the sea calmed down. Those able to assembled on deck to see some whales. I felt quite ill but seeing those wonderful creatures lifted my spirits a lot.

"The crew and nursing staff were excellent. I spent most of my time on the upper deck which was rather beautiful. I lived on hot Bovril and water biscuits - my poor stomach could not take anything else.

"Being on deck for so long, I had the privilege of seeing an iceberg with a polar bear on it – I shall never forget that. We were a couple of days late to our destination of Halifax Nova Scotia. I was below deck when I

heard a shout and the ship's siren. I rushed on deck with the others and a sailor shouted: 'Land Ahoy'. I was so glad, hopefully to see my dear husband after so long. The voyage took seven days instead of five.

"One thing I will never forget is the sight of a young man waiting at the dock. We were told that he had been waiting for six months for his bride watching every ship that came into dock.

"I often wonder if she finally got to Canada."

PACKED IN

Canadian troops crowded on Aquitania's deck, towards the end of World War II

LAST VOYAGE

Stripped of her lifeboats and framed by tug boat smoke, Aquitania is canted away from the Southampton quayside where well-wishers bid farewell for her final sailing to the Scottish shipbreakers, on February 18, 1950

"A vessel of truly remarkable character had left the centre stage of Britain's mercantile marine after 36 years"

SCRATCH CREW

Top, Master, officers and shipping reporters pose for a souvenir group photo on Aquitania's aft boat deck. Above, Capt RGB Woolatt (centre) Quartermaster Roberts (right) and Carpenter J Elder, link arms for the liner's send-off. Left, Mr Elder, of Glasgow, who served on the liner for 30 years, rings the ship's bell, on February 18, 1950

CENTENARY IN THE CITY

Aquitania set the tone for Cunard's standards of luxurious service and attention to detail which remains today

AQUITANIA'S legacy remains a strong presence in the current Cunard fleet, even if ship shapes and interior designs have changed out of all recognition.

The changing economic climate of the 1920s-30s, which created the need for Aquitania to mix transatlantic crossings with cruises, is one that set the template for Cunard's flagship RMS Queen Mary 2 to follow closely.

Of all the great North Atlantic shipping lines, Cunard is the only survivor still committed to a scheduled passenger service between Europe and North America.

That lineage also strongly descends from Aquitania to QM2, via firstly Queen Mary (I) of 1936, Queen Elizabeth (I) of 1940, and Queen Elizabeth 2 (QE2) of 1967.

Although their looks have greatly evolved, there is a distinct family resemblance, emphasised by the same colour scheme of black hulls, white superstructure and Cunard's historic orange-red funnels with black tops and thin black bands (albeit reduced in each generation from four to three to two to one stack).

Not only have interiors become more spacious over this century of ocean liner development (QM2 is three times the volume of Aquitania), but there has been a switch from the pre-WWI fashion for historic styles to a more streamlined ocean liner Art Deco style.

However, as this was introduced by Queen Mary (I) in the mid-1930s, it could be argued that her contemporary namesake QM2 also keys into that same British desire to combine modernity with a romantic past ambience, just as Aquitania did.

The arrival of Cunard's MS Queen Victoria in Liverpool on May 30-31, 2014,

for the first overnight stay by one of the company's ships since 1968, is a very fitting way to celebrate Aquitania's centenary in the city, the birthplace of Cunard in 1840. Then next year QM2 will undertake the first transatlantic crossing from Liverpool to New York (via Halifax, NS; and Boston, Mass) in 46 years as part of Cunard Line's 175th anniversary events.

Both Queen Victoria and QM2 will be berthed at Liverpool Cruise Terminal, the very place (back then it was Princes Landing Stage) from which Aquitania left on her maiden voyage on May 30, 1914 for the start of a brilliant career and one which was unsurpassed by any previous ocean liner and unrepeatable by any future passenger ship.

POSTWAR RULERS

Above, the stern of RMS Queen Elizabeth (I) in King George V Graving Dock, Southampton, showing her Liverpool port of registry. Right, a great aerial shot of her running mate, RMS Queen Mary (I) dressed overall and getting up speed

"The Cunard lineage strongly descends from Aquitania to QM2, via Queen Mary, Queen Elizabeth and the QE2"

MERSEY QUEEN

Above, RMS Queen Elizabeth 2, known universally as QE2, makes her Liverpool debut in 1990 to mark Cunard Line's 150th anniversary at its original home. Lower, some 18 years later, QE2 arrives for her farewell visit in 2008

SHIP SHAPE

Paul Louden-Brown, ocean liner historian, (pictured above) says: "The Cunard Building is Aquitania ashore. The fact both had Arthur Davis as interior designer and date from 1914 is not coincidental. "If you want to see what Aquitania looked like inside, take a tour of the magnificent Cunard Building." Left, an Egyptian style corridor recalls the liner's swimming pool decor and right, a fireplace could be one in her Carolean Smoking Room. Above are spare keys from long lost Cunard liners, still in the safe room

MERSEY RETURN

The Queen Victoria during a visit to Merseyside in 2010, watched by one of Sir Antony Gormley's 'Iron Men' on Crosby beach

Historic Queen Victoria visit to mark centenary

MICHAEL Gallagher, Cunard Line Public Relations Manager & Historian, said: "It's fair to say that every Cunard ship is special and it's fair to say that some Cunarders are perhaps more special than others.

"The Queens, past and present, for sure have made their mark.

"And so did the much-loved Aquitania. Her records of sailing more miles than any other and being the longest-serving Cunard express liner stood for decades eventually exceeded by QE2.

"Wartime Prime Minister Winston Churchill credited the contribution of Aquitania, as well the Queens, in the Second World War for shortening the conflict in Europe by a year.

"Having Queen Victoria berthed at Liverpool on May 30, 2014, and making the first overnight in the city by a Cunard passenger ship in almost 50 years, is evidence of Cunard's desire to celebrate Aquitania's Maiden Voyage departure 100 years earlier and her unique contribution to the company's history.

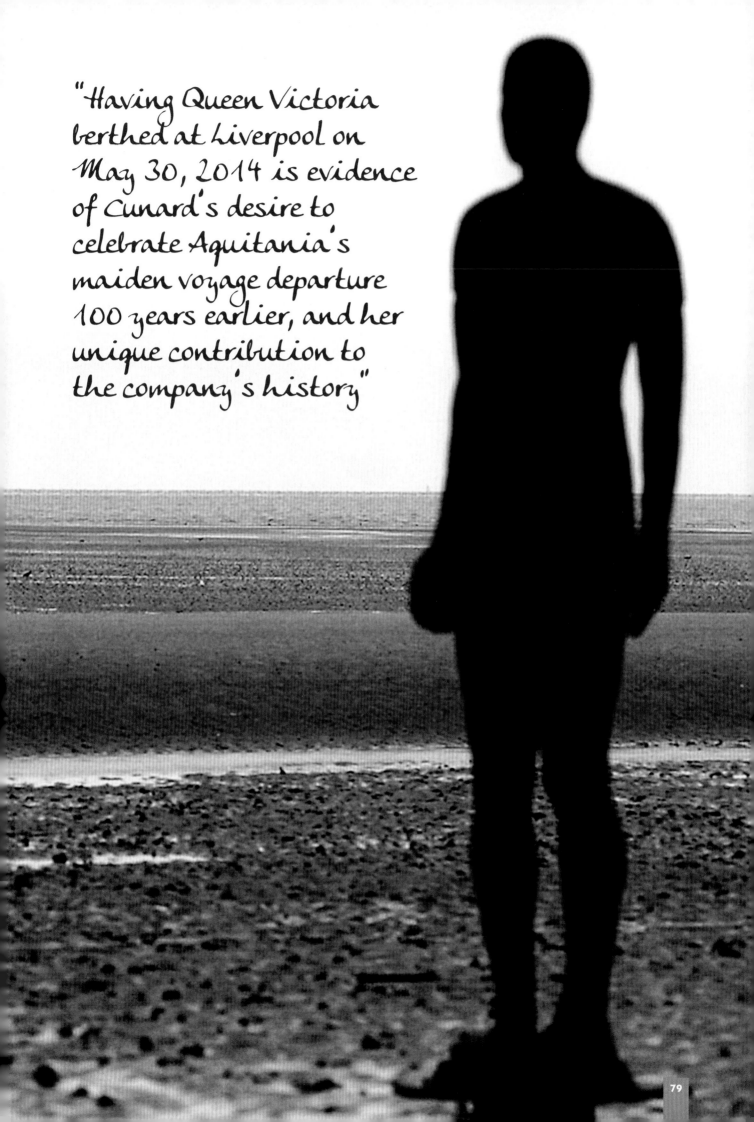

"Having Queen Victoria berthed at Liverpool on May 30, 2014 is evidence of Cunard's desire to celebrate Aquitania's maiden voyage departure 100 years earlier, and her unique contribution to the company's history"

DARK LADY

Aquitania's huge size appears emphasised, not diminished, as she rises up into the night sky while in Southampton's Floating Dry Dock during a refit in the 1930s

"Aquitania had such classical elegance, both inside and out, that she was the inspiration for the design of just about every Cunarder for the next 20 years"
William H Miller Jnr, ocean liner historian

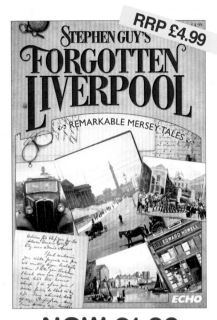

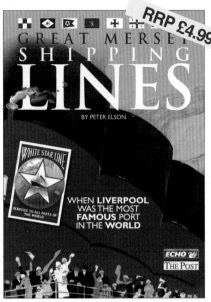
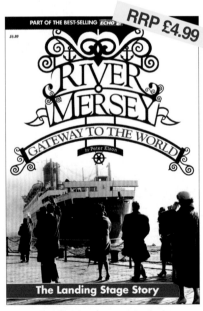
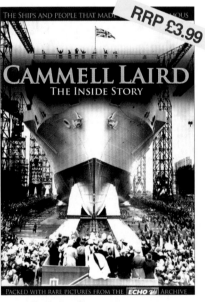
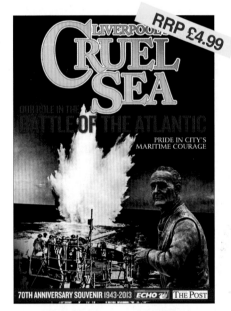